Insane Energy for Lazy People

A Complete System for Becoming Incredibly Energetic

Andrii Sedniev

Insane Energy for Lazy People

A Complete System for Becoming Incredibly Energetic

Published by Andrii Sedniev

Copyright © 2019 by Andrii Sedniev

ISBN 978-1-07440-265-5

First printing, 2019

www.AndriiSedniev.com

PRINTED IN THE UNITED STATES OF AMERICA

Dedications

This book and my love are dedicated to Olena, my wife and partner, who makes every day in life worthwhile. Thank you for supporting me on every stage of development of *Insane Energy for Lazy People* and giving encouragement when I needed it the most. Without you, this book might never have been finished.

I also want to dedicate this book to all past students of *Insane Energy for Lazy People* who by their success inspire me to become a better person every day.

Contents

The most energetic man in the world

In order to change anything in the world you need energy, and the more energy you have in your internal battery the more positive impact you can make on your life and the lives of other people. You can't increase the amount of hours in a day but you can increase the quality of these hours by raising your energy level. Personal energy is the most valuable currency in the world, which you can transform to success, money and happiness.

Many years ago I was sitting in my house watching the rain outside the window and thinking about how sad my life had become. Within a day I accomplished on average about 30 minutes' worth of work, because keeping focus on a task long enough was difficult. I couldn't survive the entire day without an after lunch nap, because after a couple of hours of wakefulness I felt sleepy. I was 60 pounds overweight, struggled to take a long walk and sometimes even to take a deep full breath. My energy was at a historical minimum and the worst part was that I was only 25 years old. In the middle of my thoughts I heard a call and noticed that it was my friend Jason.

I have met many people who were satisfied with their lives, but nobody as happy as Jason. In his 48 years, he has built a company that made him a multimillionaire, lived happily for 25 years with his wife, traveled around the world for 365 days, climbed Mt. Everest, won a national dancing competition and if I continue this list we will have enough material for several adventure novels. But what impressed me the most about Jason was the happiness that he radiates.

When he speaks he is always smiling, he is passionate about life and genuinely interested in the person he talks to, and this energy of happiness is contagious.

Jason asked: "Hi, Andrii. How is it going? I will be in your town on the weekend. Would you like to meet with me somewhere in a café to chat for a couple of hours?"

I said: "Sounds awesome. Of course I would love to meet. By the way I wanted to ask you one thing. I struggle with extremely low energy level and can't understand what is going on. When I was a kid I had an enormous amount of energy and felt that I could move mountains. Right now I am 25, have no energy at all, and feel like I am very old. I think that you are the most energetic man in the world, how do you manage to have such an active life at 48?"

Jaison said: "Don't worry, Andrii. Around your age I felt the same way but after understanding several concepts and going through several life experiences I learned how to manage energy effectively and bring it to a maximum level. Right now I need to go to a meeting with partners, but on the weekend I will share with you everything I know about energy."

Based on ideas I learned from Jason, based on 10 years of research of the most energetic people in the world, and based on experiments on my students, I have created an *Insane Energy for Lazy People* system. The goal of this system is to maximize your personal energy level and to significantly increase the amount of happiness in your life. Once you learn the ideas from this system and implement them in your life, you will feel like you have a jet engine inside and can accomplish within a day many times more than an average person. Becoming energetic is one of the most valuable presents that you can give yourself because it will have a

2

positive impact on all areas of your life, and you will experience more joyful moments of which happiness consists.

If you want to fulfill a dream – you need energy. If you want to feel great physically and emotionally – you need energy. If you want to build good relationships with other people – you need energy. The more energy you have inside, the more fulfilled and colorful your life is. Are you ready to take a trip through a land of Insane Energy and to upgrade your internal engine? Let's go.

"The world belongs to the energetic." – Ralph Waldo Emerson

Happiness is progress

On Saturday just as agreed Jason and I met in a café. After a waiter gave us menus and we talked about our lives for a couple of minutes we got into a discussion of happiness. Jason said: "The reason why many people aren't happy in their lives is that they don't clearly understand what happiness is. People know that happiness is something pleasurable, they know that happiness is when they have a good mood, they know that happiness is what everybody wants, but they don't clearly understand what happiness is.

"Here is the definition: 'Happiness is the emotion of progress towards a desirable goal.' Basically if you have a goal that you are passionate about, and you feel that you are making progress towards it, you are happy. It's important to understand that happiness isn't related to actually achieving a goal, but it's related to making progress towards a goal.

"When you have achieved a goal, no matter how big it was, you experience a short-term happiness boost. A week after you purchased an expensive car, were accepted by an Ivy League university or got a promotion at work – these things become a normal part of your life and don't bring joy anymore. There is a special term – hedonic adaptation – which describes how people get used to any amount of wealth, to any achievement or any experience, and their happiness returns to a regular level. When you were a kid very simple things made you happy – an ice cream, a toy or an amusement park – but when you become an adult you already have eaten thousands of ice creams, played with hundreds of toys and visited dozens of amusement parks, and these things don't bring as much joy as before. As an adult to feel better you travel around the world, eat in expensive restaurants, buy a house, jump from a parachute, but after some time these things also become victims of hedonic adaptation.

"The only thing that can bring happiness steadily and long term is regular progress towards a desirable goal. When you experience small successes on the way to a goal the chemical called dopamine is released in your body. Dopamine is responsible for feelings of pleasure and motivation to take actions on the way to a goal. The more progress you make, the more dopamine is released, the more dopamine is released, the happier you feel and the more motivated you are to make even more progress. Because of dopamine, progress is the strongest motivation in the world and if you want to be energetic you need to regularly experience small successes on the way to a desirable goal.

"Harvard researchers Teresa Amabile and Steven Kramer in their experiment analyzed 12,000 daily surveys filled out by 238 individuals from 7 companies over a span of 4 months. It was discovered that the biggest driver for positive emotions, high motivation level, and good mood was the amount of progress that participants made in work that was meaningful for them."

I looked at Jason and said: "Sounds interesting. I have never thought about happiness this way."

Jason looked at me, smiled and continued. "Now that you know that happiness is an emotion of progress towards a desirable goal, I will share with you two important principles that help to maximize happiness.

"Firstly, after you achieve a goal, no matter how big it was, a short period of euphoria will be followed by depression or apathy if you don't set the next ambitious goal. Dreams should grow faster than you reach them, and even before accomplishing a current goal you need to have in mind the next goal to make sure that the cycle 'progress, success, dopamine, happiness, progress' is never suspended.

"Secondly, you need to take massive action towards a goal to make fast progress. Successful people work hard not because they are workaholics, but because massive action increases the amount of progress that they experience during a day and as a result more dopamine is released in the body and they become happier.

"All people are positive emotions addicts and strive to regularly experience moments of happiness. It's important to take massive action to speed up progress towards a goal, and it is important every evening to remember small successes you have made during the day to increase your dopamine level and motivation to act. If progress is slow, your brain will seek positive emotions elsewhere, for example in unhealthy food, movies or computer games which will distract you from work and slow down progress even further. In our lives we stand on an escalator that slowly moves down towards apathy and depression, so if you want to maintain a good mood you need to walk up fast and sometimes even run.

"If I were to give only one recommendation about how to increase energy it would be this: Always have a desirable goal in front of you and take massive action to make progress towards this goal as fast as possible." When Jason noticed a waiter approaching our table he said: "We are ready to make an order."

I always tell people if you want to know the secret to happiness, I can give it to you in one word: progress. — Tony Robbins

Happiness comes to those who are moving toward something they want very much to happen. — Earl Nightingale

People have two problems. Dreams that they haven't fulfilled and dreams that they have fulfilled. — Anonymous.

Happiness is anticipation of a near upcoming success. — Andrey Onistrat

The power of goals

To be energetic you need to have a compelling future to look forward to so that you are excited to make progress towards it every day. Lack of goals leads to apathy, degradation and depression. Presence of long-term and short-term goals increases level of motivation, energy and happiness.

Pump a goal with energy

Firstly, for a goal to have any strength, make sure that it's not a goal set by your wife, set by your friends or set by your parents — but it's a goal that is meaningful for you. When answering the question: "Why do I want to achieve this goal?" you need to have a strong reason that will motivate you to take action after waking up in the morning. Only goals that are meaningful for you have big energy and charge your internal battery when you make progress towards them.

Secondly, any goal that has a deadline has more energy behind it than a goal without a deadline. Numerous studies have proven that if you work towards a goal that has a deadline it is achieved at least 1.5 times faster. The faster you achieve intermediate goals, the more motivation you have to work towards a long-term goal, and the faster you achieve further intermediate goals. Even if your goal doesn't have a deadline set by circumstances, set a self-imposed deadline to pump a goal with energy and speed up progress.

Presence of goals is perhaps the biggest energy generator that you can use. However for goals to have high energy, make sure that these goals are meaningful for you and that they have deadlines even if self-imposed.

150 wishes technique

Create a list of 150 wishes that you would like to fulfill on a piece of paper or in a text file where around 100 are quick and easy wishes (for example to lose a pound of weight, to do 100 pushups, to clean the house), 40 are average wishes, and 10 are big and seemingly impossible wishes. Every time you fulfill a wish cross it off from the list and say: "I wanted it and I achieved it." When you experience success and acknowledge it, dopamine is released in the body and your motivation to succeed again increases dramatically. When you fulfill your small wishes you begin building a success momentum that allows you to fulfill average wishes, and when you fulfill average wishes the success momentum turns into a success avalanche that will allow you to fulfill big wishes. Stretch your mind and write down in a wish list everything that you would want if there were no limitations, say if you were a billionaire who had all the talents and resources in the world.

Our wheel of life consists of the following areas: career, self-development, relationships and socialization, health, hobbies. If one of these areas is significantly weaker than others, then it negatively affects results in other areas, the wheel rolls poorly and happiness suffers. When you select your small, average and big wishes, make sure that you have at least several wishes in each of the five categories. Also remember to revisit your wish list from time to time and remove the wishes that you have fulfilled or don't want anymore and add new wishes that you realized you want. The faster you fulfill old wishes, the more motivation you have to make progress and the faster new wishes will come to your mind.

Goals are the biggest source of energy that is available to us, so make sure that you not only have a big list of wishes but also that these things are meaningful for you and have deadlines.

You need to work on your goals professionally and with full immersion.
— Andrey Onistrat

Social connections for energy

Many years ago I attended a leadership training conducted by Vadym, a famous Russian psychologist. One particular exercise impressed me so much that I clearly remember it to this day. Vadym picked a volunteer to stand at the spot in the middle of the room and asked all other members of the training to form a semicircle around this spot, to point a finger at the volunteer, and synchronously say: "You are awesome! You are very good-looking! You are extremely smart! You have an excellent sense of humor! Your voice is magnificent! You have the best ideas! On a scale from 1 to 10, you are 11! Colors seem brighter when you're around. Thanks for being you!" When it was my turn to stand in the middle of the semicircle and other training members pointed their fingers at me and said all these phrases, my mood was raised and I felt more energetic. I thought: "Wow, all these people weren't sincere because they simply did what Vadym told them to, but I still I felt awesome!" That day I understood how social interactions can significantly affect our sense of happiness.

When you hug your spouse, shake hands with a colleague, talk to a friend, or just hang around other people, a pleasure-inducing hormone, oxytocin, is released to your bloodstream which impacts the brain's serotonin production. Serotonin is an important neurotransmitter that contributes to our feelings of happiness and well-being. The more high-quality social interactions you experience, the happier you are.

According to the European Social Survey people who never meet socially with friends, relatives or colleagues on average rate their happiness 4.9 on a 10 point scale. People who meet socially once a week rate their happiness 7.2 and people who meet socially every day rate their happiness on average 7.6. Perhaps even more important than frequency of social interactions is quality of these interactions. According to the European Social Survey people who don't have anyone who they can discuss intimate or personal matters with rate their happiness 6 on a 10 point scale. People who have 3 people they can discuss intimate or personal matters with rate their happiness 7.5 and people who have more than 10 such people rate their happiness 8.1. It was scientifically proven that the correlation between social connections and happiness is bigger than the correlation between happiness and money, happiness and fame, or happiness and education. People are designed to be social, so we need to regularly communicate with others to be happy.

 If happiness is the emotion of progress towards a desirable goal, then social connections are an amplifier of happiness that you already have. Every person experiences ups and downs that can make them happy or upset. Your social support group reduces the amount of stress that you experience during downs and helps to recover from them faster. At the same time, the social support group makes your ups more pleasurable and meaningful when you talk about your happiness with other people. In order to improve a social impact on your happiness, you need to begin by creating a fulfilling marriage, developing relationships with friends, and growing a circle of people who you occasionally communicate with.

Also remember that social connections are a two-sided sword. On one side, positive communication can fill you with energy and happiness; on the other side, negative communication can drain energy out of you and make you unhappy. Every person who you talk to either fills you with energy or reduces your energy, and rarely does the energy stay on the same level. One of the most effective ways to become happier is to increase the amount of interaction with positive people in your life and reduce interaction with negative people. If you want to become more energetic you need to invest time and effort in developing your own social network of people who you can talk to and exchange positive energy with.

If you notice that your mood is down, you may use these social interaction techniques that are quick to implement and release serotonin in the body:

1. Meet new people that you share the same goal with: become a volunteer, join a club, play a team sport, find a job, take foreign language classes.

2. Interaction with animals can instantly make you feel better. Go horseback riding, swim with dolphins or just stroke a pet. If you don't have a pet you can get the same positive emotions by stroking somebody else's pet.

3. Go to a concert, a show or a sports competition. Engaging in experiences in a collective way raises mood and boosts feeling of happiness.

4. Go to a coffee house, to a shopping mall, to a gym or to a library. You don't even have to interact with people there, just being in the same physical space with other people can help you to reset your mind and improve mood.

To build a long-lasting happiness and to raise the average level of energy, it's important to have a fulfilling marriage and to build a social network consisting of family members, friends and colleagues who you can regularly communicate with. Talking to people who you like and who like you feels good, and these interactions can help you to reduce stress when you fail and increase pleasure when you succeed. Developing and strengthening relationships in your social network is definitely worth time and effort because it has one of the biggest impacts on your level of energy and happiness.

If I wanted to predict your happiness and I could only know one thing about you, I wouldn't want to know about your gender, religion, health, or income. I'd want to know about the strength of your relationships with your friends and family... – Daniel Gilbert

Loneliness kills. It's as powerful as smoking or alcoholism. – Robert Waldinger

Charge a body with energy

The daily amount of energy that you can spend depends on four components: exercise, weight, sleep and nutrition. The more you exercise, the less overweight you are, the better you sleep, the healthier you eat, the more energetic you feel. What is interesting is that all these components affect each other: If you exercise more you have better metabolism and better weight, you sleep better, your appetite is suppressed, and you eat less unhealthy food. If you eat healthy food – you lose weight, you sleep better, you can exercise easier. If you have a perfect weight – you can exercise easier, you have less desire to eat unhealthy food, and you have a better sleep. If you have a better sleep – your metabolism improves and you lose extra weight, you have less desire to eat unhealthy food, and you have more energy to exercise. The real magic happens when you do all these things together: you exercise, you sleep well, you eat healthy food and you maintain perfect weight. In this case your energy skyrockets and you can do and experience more within a day that other people can within a week.

Exercise for energy

In 1999 psychologist James Blumenthal conducted a study at Duke University to analyze the effect of exercise on adults suffering from depression. During the four-month experiment 156 adults were split into 3 groups. The first group exercised for 45 minutes three times a week, the second group took antidepressant medication, the third group did a combination of both. At the end of the experiment it turned out that all 3 groups experienced the same improvement in happiness which showed that exercise was equally effective as antidepressant medication. Scientists conducting other studies have confirmed that physically active people have more pleasant-activated feelings than people who aren't physically active. Moreover, people have more pleasant-activated feelings on days when they are more physically active than usual.

When you exercise, the body experiences stress and a happiness hormone called endorphins is released that interacts with receptors in your brain that reduce perception of pain. Endorphins not only help to alleviate stress but also raise your mood and feeling of happiness. Our brain is connected with our body, and the way you handle your body affects your emotions, mood and energy. Remember that it's close to impossible to stay depressed if you regularly exercise and stand under a shower of endorphins. No matter how much stress you experience in life, exercises help the brain to rest and replace the feeling of anxiety with the feeling of joy.

Researchers at Saginaw Valley State University in Michigan analyzed grades and exercises of 266 undergraduate students. They found that students who regularly participated in vigorous physical activities on average had a 0.4 points higher G.P.A. on a 4.0 grade scale than those who didn't exercise.

When you exercise, blood flow to the brain is increased, which nourishes the brain and makes it better at thinking creatively and concentrating on a task without distractions. Many studies confirm that the brain part that is responsible for thinking and memory has greater volume in the heads of people who exercise compared to people who don't. Our brain is constructed in a way that it needs external stimulation for optimal performance, and exercising is excellent at stimulating the brain.

Imagine that your body is a battery and the more energy this battery can store, the more energy you will be able to have within a day. Every night when you sleep this battery is recharged, however exactly for the amount of energy that you spent during the previous day. If you want to have a lot of energy tomorrow, you need to spend a lot of energy today. Our brain consumes only 20% of energy, so it's a must to supplement thinking activities with walking and exercises that spend a lot of energy, so that your internal battery has more energy tomorrow. Your body accumulates as much energy as you need: for thinking, for moving, for exercising. The more active you are today, the more energy you spend today and the more energy you will have to burn tomorrow. Exercises give you more energy and keep you from feeling listless.

The older you get, the more critical physical exercises are for maintaining high quality of life. Physical activity is one of the main sources of energy and if you want to be happy and successful you need to exercise regularly. Make physical exercises your habit like brushing your teeth, taking a shower or eating breakfast, and being inside your body will be more comfortable.

When you are young, fitness is a sport. As you grow older, it's a necessity. — T. Boone Pickens

Staying as fit as possible is the key to everything. — Michael Moritz

When it comes to mood, the effects of exercise may only last about 24 hours. — Teresa Gevedon

Sedya fitness

There are people who regularly jog, there are people who regularly pump muscles at a gym, there are people who regularly do yoga and all of them aren't gaining maximum value from exercising because aerobic exercises, muscle exercises and stretching provide different benefits for a body. Based on many years of research I have developed a training concept called "Sedya fitness" that allows you to exercise with the maximum benefit for energy. Sedya fitness basically means that when you exercise you need to devote approximately 60% of time to aerobic exercises, 20% of time to training muscles, and 20% to stretching. This approach will maximize your level of energy and happiness. When you engage all three of these components of exercises (aerobic, muscles, stretching) your body is in an optimal shape and you gain as much value from workouts as possible. You might ask: "How much do I need to exercise?" It depends on your goals and current fitness level, but it should be in a range between 3 times per week for 1 hour and 5 times per week for 1.5 hours. If your aim besides energy is also to lose weight then you might need to exercise more often and the workouts should be longer.

Aerobic exercises are exercises when you sweat and your heart rate increases, for example: swimming, running, cycling, aerobics, dancing. Aerobic exercises are extremely effective at burning fat and suppressing appetite which allows you to lose weight or avoid gaining weight. Aerobic exercises improve blood flow and cell nourishment by oxygen which increases your energy level. Aerobic exercises also release endorphins that help to cope with stress and improve mood. Dancing is especially effective at improving mood because doing aerobic exercises and listening to music both release endorphins in your body.

Exercises for muscles increase metabolism in the body, which improves processing of calories and as a result helps to maintain a perfect weight. Muscle exercises also strengthen muscles, bones, joints and ligaments, improving your body strength, stamina and energy. The most effective exercises for energy purposes are exercises with your own body weight such as pushups, pull-ups, planks, squats or exercising the abdominals.

Stretching exercises such as yoga and Pilates make the body more flexible, stretch the spine, improve posture and increase elasticity of stiff muscles and mobility of joints. Stretching exercises also give a lot of benefits that muscle and aerobic exercises give such as increased metabolism, stress relief, improved sleep and energy.

When during a workout you do aerobic exercises, muscle exercises and stretching, you get much more value from exercise than a person who does just aerobic exercises, just muscle exercises or just stretching. To get even more happiness and energy in addition to exercising you also need to have an active lifestyle and walk at least 10,000 steps per day. Simply walking more helps to lose weight, improves heart health, increases self-esteem, tones muscles, increases metabolism, reduces stress, improves mood, increases energy and strengthens bones and joints. If you feel depressed or your productivity dropped – go for a walk and most likely when you return your mood and productivity will increase. The sedentary lifestyle with little movement is as dangerous for health as smoking or drinking alcohol. Nature has designed the human body so that you need to regularly engage all muscles and move. Motion is health, motion is energy and motion is happiness.

Besides exercises and walking there are also physical pleasures that can improve your mood and energy level: contrast shower, massage, sauna, sex with a spouse and hugging people you like. Massage boosts serotonin and dopamine levels responsible for the feeling of happiness and decreases the stress hormone cortisol. A contrast shower and sauna increase energy, uplift mood and improve blood circulation. Regular sex with a spouse reduces stress, improves overall physical fitness and releases endorphins which reduce stress and improve feelings of happiness. Finally, hugging people you like releases serotonin and endorphin to blood vessels to boost the feeling of happiness and negate sadness. If you occasionally take a contrast shower, get a massage, go to a sauna, have sex with a spouse and hug people you like, you will make a great contribution to your average level of energy and happiness.

The Sedya fitness concept helps to get maximum energy and happiness from their major supplier – physical activities. To get maximum energy, health and happiness from exercises, make sure that you do a combination of aerobic exercises, muscle training exercises and stretching exercises during your workout. Develop a habit of walking on average 10,000 steps per day and taking regular walking breaks in long sitting streaks. Add to this a list of pleasures that you indulge in, such as a contrast shower, massage, sauna, sex with a spouse and hugging people that you like. Exercises, 10,000 steps and physical pleasures will take your energy to a level that many people can only dream about.

Nutrition and food for energy

When I was 28 I went through a particularly stressful period in my life and I ate chocolates and other tasty food to uplift my mood and to make myself feel better. The more I ate the more pounds I gained, the more pounds I gained, the more stressed and frustrated I became and the more I ate until I earned 50 extra pounds. One day I went out with my wife for a walk and I realized: "Oh my goodness, I can't breathe. My stomach doesn't allow me to take a full breath, I can only sip some air with my nose, but I can't take a full breath with a full chest like I always could." By this time my productivity was at a historic minimum, I was depressed and I felt sleepy the entire day and needed to have a long nap in the middle of the day to function at least somehow. But when I realized that I couldn't even take a full breath with my entire chest it was the last straw. My wife, Olena, said: "We will begin to exercise 5 times per week and will completely change the way we eat." After a series of experiments on our bodies we have developed a nutrition system that not only increases productivity but also makes you feel extremely energetic and as a bonus you lose all extra pounds that you have gained without significant effort. Within a year of starting to follow this nutrition system I have lost all my 50 pounds, I have as much energy as when I was a teenager and my productivity and feeling of happiness significantly increased. I remember how I felt myself at 28 as a nightmare and promised myself to never go back to this weight.

The first thing I discovered is that the food that makes you productive, the food that allows you to lose weight and the food that improves your level of happiness is exactly the same food. The second thing I discovered was that improving the quality of nutrition and raising the amount of energy that you get from food is easy if you understand a couple of simple concepts.

Our body has a parameter called pH balance which represents a balance between alkaline and acid inside our blood system. Each food that we eat has its own pH level that ranges between 0 and 14. Everything that is above 7 is alkaline and is considered healthy, and everything below 7 is acid and is considered unhealthy. A healthy human body should have blood pH that is slightly alkaline somewhere between 7.35 and 7.45. In order to achieve this range about 60% of the food you consume should be alkaline such as broccoli, spinach or avocado, however the problem is that the majority of people eat too much acid food such as hamburgers, cookies or chocolates and as a result their pH level is below the optimal level. This condition is called acidosis.

Here is a small list of problems that eating too much unhealthy acid food can create: low energy and chronic fatigue, weight gain, premature aging, tendency to get infections, loss of enthusiasm, depressive tendencies, headaches, easily stressed, gastritis, osteoporosis and joint pain.

In general any food or drink that you consume can fall into four categories: highly acid, acid, alkaline and highly alkaline or if you wish highly unhealthy, unhealthy, healthy and highly healthy. In order to significantly improve your pH level and increase not only your energy but also your health you need to add to your diet more highly alkaline (highly healthy) food and significantly reduce consumption of highly alkaline (highly unhealthy) food. And don't worry too much about alkaline (healthy) or acid (unhealthy) categories, you can eat them as you do now because if you take care of the extreme categories you will have made already a significant positive impact on your pH balance. Below I will share with you principles that made an enormous change in my weight and energy level.

As I said, you need to eliminate highly unhealthy food from your diet and add highly healthy food to improve the pH balance in your blood system. You might ask: "How exactly can I do this?" I would say do the following: "Substitute red meat such as veal, beef and pork with chicken and fish. Substitute all drinks such as coffee, juices or alcohol with pure water and green tea. Eliminate from your diet as much as possible highly acid food such as: pastry, cookies, chocolate, mayonnaise. And add more highly alkaline food such as: spinach, broccoli, lettuce, dates, apples, pears, zucchini and other vegetables and fruits. I guarantee you if you will just follow the recommendations in this paragraph you will feel more energetic, however if you want to become even more advanced in your nutrition simply look for a pH table for various foods and decide for yourself what you need to eat more and less. Remember that you don't need to worry about every single food that you eat, but your goal is to improve overall pH balance and for this you need just to shift the balance between unhealthy and healthy food that you eat.

In terms of energy people enjoy unhealthy food such as sweets, burgers or coffee because they quickly raise the level of sugar in the body which raises mood and energy for a short period of time. After this short-term mood and energy increase, the sugar level drops below the average level. Your mood and energy get worse than before eating unhealthy food, and this drop is long term. Basically the unhealthy food allows you to increase your mood and energy above your regular level for a few minutes, and in exchange after these few minutes your mood and energy drop below your average level for several hours. As you can see, it's much better to avoid such energy spikes caused by unhealthy food and work on increasing your average energy level through other means.

The best drink that exists is water as it is not only extremely healthy but also improves your energy. Water reduces hunger and increases metabolism which allows you to maintain perfect weight. Water boosts the work of the brain and increases your energy level. In addition water helps to get rid of toxins inside the body through sweat and urine. If you want to be energetic increase the daily amount of water that you drink and substitute the majority of other drinks that you consume with water.

I recommend that you not eat after 6 p.m. if you go to bed at midnight. Digestion after 6 p.m. is significantly slower than during the day and if you eat supper say at 9 p.m. the food won't digest by the time you sleep and will stay in your stomach at night. As a result you will gain extra weight and will get a not very deep sleep which will affect your productivity the next day. Also when you eat breakfast, lunch and supper make sure that you don't overeat; you should have a feeling of lightness after you leave the table. If you finish eating with a feeling: "Oh, I have eaten so much that I even struggle to breathe," all your energy will be directed to digestion and for a couple of hours after breakfast, lunch or supper you might feel sleepy and will struggle to work with high concentration and be productive.

In summary if you want to become more productive and energetic follow these tips: Reduce the amount of highly unhealthy food and increase the amount of highly healthy food that you eat, drink more water, don't eat after 6 p.m. and don't overeat during breakfast, lunch and supper. According to research conducted by the International Labor Organization in 2015, poor diet is costing countries around the world up to 20% in lost productivity. If noticeably improving your productivity and quality of life requires only making couple of simple changes in your eating habits, why not do them right now? Remember that what you eat, how much you eat and when you eat has a significant impact on your health and energy level.

Weight loss

Imagine that you enter a gym and take one 25-pound dumbbell in your left hand and another 25-pound dumbbell in your right hand. Now try to run with these dumbbells, try to jump with them or try to dance with them. Heavy, aren't they? If you get tired from walking with two 25-pound dumbbells you can put them down, however if you have 50 pounds of extra weight on you, unfortunately you will have to carry this weight every day 24/7.

You can make an enormous impact on your average energy level if you figure out your perfect weight range and then through healthy nutrition and exercises get your weight to this range. If you have many extra pounds on you right now, it may take some time to get rid of them, but it's one of the biggest presents that you can give yourself because having a perfect weight will improve significantly your self-confidence, mood, sleep, metabolism, health and life satisfaction. When you reach your perfect weight you will feel lightness and being in your excellent body will bring you joy and happiness.

When you reach the age of 30 your base metabolism drops and you may notice that even if you have the same lifestyle as when you were 18 now you are gaining weight. People who are in good physical shape after age 30 are usually eating very healthy food and exercising regularly to maintain weight in a perfect range. These people know that the body no longer forgives mistakes in conducting a healthy lifestyle that it forgave at a younger age. The Institute for Health Metrics and Evaluation has estimated that roughly 30% of children in the USA are overweight, however among adults because of the lower metabolism and sedentary lifestyle 66% are overweight. The older you get the more important it is to eat healthy, exercise and have an active lifestyle.

Many people who begin working on losing weight during the first week or two decide that it's very difficult to eat less and to load their heavy body with exercises. In fact it's difficult only at the beginning and with each pound that you lose it will become easier and easier. The closer your weight is to a perfect weight the better is your metabolism, the smaller is the serving of food that will satisfy your hunger, the smaller is the volume of your stomach, the better is your sleep and the more energy you have. It's fair to estimate that with each pound you lose that gets you closer to your perfect weight you become 2% more energetic throughout the day. So if you have for example 50 pounds of extra weight it's a huge hole through which you are losing energy, and if you can cover it by losing this weight your average energy level will at least double.

If you compare a fight between lightweight boxers with a fight between heavyweight boxers you will see that lightweight boxers are moving faster, they are throwing significantly more punches, they are more energetic. If you compare short-distance runners to long-distance runners you will notice that long-distance runners are slimmer and can endure a physical load significantly longer. The same is true not only in sports, but also in everyday life – people who are at their perfect weight are more physically active during a day, they can endure both physical and intellectual load longer and they are significantly more energetic than people who are carrying "heavy dumbbells" on them. To be highly energetic you need to be strong and light so it's critical to get your weight to a perfect range if it's not yet there. In the next section we will discuss several interesting concepts that are extremely effective for losing weight or maintaining it in a perfect range.

How to lose weight effectively

If you want to lose weight you simply need to spend more calories per day than you consume. We consume calories by eating food and spend calories by moving, exercising and thinking. You are consuming calories even when you eat very healthy food, but considerably less than when you eat unhealthy food. You spend calories even when you watch TV or sleep, but considerably less than when you go for a walk or exercise. Basically if you are gaining weight right now it means that you are consuming more calories than you are spending. To begin losing weight you need to eat less food, and make sure that food that you eat is healthy. At the same time, you need to spend more calories on movement by walking more during the day and exercising more. If you lose weight too quickly, for example if you are losing more than 2.5 pounds per week, it may be unhealthy because your body won't be able to adapt at such a fast pace. The perfect speed for losing weight is between 1 and 2.5 pounds per week.

One important concept to understand for effective weight loss is that your body doesn't need food, it only needs nutrients. When your body decides that it needs, for example, potassium, B12, copper, water and magnesium it screams: "I am hungry." You feel hungry and eat a hamburger, French fries and a soft drink. After the meal your body doesn't see any nutrients coming and screams again: "Hey, I am still hungry! I need potassium, B12, copper, water and magnesium!" You feel hungry and eat a donut with coffee. Your body doesn't see any nutrients coming and screams again: "I am still hungry! I still need these nutrients." You hear this message and go eat chocolate. The message here is if the body doesn't get necessary nutrients that are contained in healthy food, you may consume a lot of calories but still feel hungry. If you drink water and eat healthy food, you will satisfy your body and get rid of the feeling of hunger by eating significantly less calories. Getting all necessary nutrients from healthy food will allow you to consume fewer calories (because healthy food is very rich with nutrients) which is incredibly important for maintaining perfect weight. If you eat healthy food that is rich with nutrients, you can eat less food and this food is digested more easily. If you eat unhealthy food, you will consume more calories to fulfill a need in nutrients at least partially from unhealthy food that contains few nutrients. Nutrient deficiency leads to regular overeating and as a result to gaining weight.

Controlling how much you eat and what you eat is even more important than how much you exercise. For example to burn the amount of calories contained in one Big Mac at McDonald's you might need to walk for about 2 hours. As you can see it's significantly easier to not eat one extra Big Mac than to take a two-hour walk. You might even see some marathon runners who are overweight because they are eating too much unhealthy food. You need to take control of how much you eat and what you eat, and after that add more movement and exercising to your life.

The first step in losing weight should be buying a scale and developing a habit of weighing your body every day in the morning. What gets measured is improved and simply being aware of how much you weigh will make you take more actions towards weight loss and your weight will improve. If you notice that your weight goes up, you may be motivated to decrease the amount of calories that you consume and increase the amount of calories that you spend. If you see that your weight goes down because of your healthy lifestyle, you might experience joy from your success and get motivation to keep on eating healthy food and exercising. Maintaining a perfect weight is a lifelong process, you need to stick to healthy eating and exercising habits even after you reach the perfect weight, because otherwise it will go up again.

A lot of food such as bananas, strawberries, nuts, tomatoes, sweets and many others release endorphins in our body which make us feel good. Many people when they are feeling sad or bored begin eating to entertain themselves and to feel better because of the endorphins that food releases in their body. Don't rely on this method of raising mood, because it is a very fast way to gain weight. Even eating a very healthy food in large amounts that your body doesn't need simply for entertainment will increase your weight which will lower your base level of energy. Remember that food isn't entertainment and you can get endorphins that make you feel good through numerous other methods in the *Insane Energy for Lazy People* system. Eat only when your body needs nourishment for proper functioning and don't eat if you aren't hungry. Remember to consume enough water as water not only is the healthiest drink that exists, but it also reduces the feeling of hunger and helps with consuming less calories.

Scientists have also proven that for maintaining a perfect weight instead of eating large portions of food 3 times per day it is better to eat moderate to small portions 5 times per day. Eating a banana, an apple or a yogurt may count as one meal out of the 5. Instead of a big breakfast, big lunch and big supper you may eat a moderate breakfast, moderate lunch and moderate supper and have two other small meals in between. Firstly, when gaps between meals are smaller, you avoid plunges in your energy level after a long time without food. Secondly, when you overeat during a particular meal your energy may go down because most of the energy will be devoted to digestion. It's worth mentioning that your brain gets a signal that nutrients are coming only about 20 minutes after you begin eating, so if you don't feel completely satisfied after a meal instead of eating more just wait another 20 minutes for the feeling of hunger to go away. When you eat smaller servings of food 5 times per day your energy is more evenly spread throughout the day, food is digested more effectively and metabolism is increased. As a result you maintain perfect weight more easily and become more energetic throughout the day.

Consider losing weight an interesting adventure, rather than a struggle, and remember that each pound lost that gets you closer to your optimal weight makes your body look nicer, improves your sleep, increases your metabolism, improves your health, gives you 2% more energy and makes your life happier. When your weight is in the perfect range, continue measuring it every morning so that if it gets out of the range you can get it back to the range with little effort.

Sleep for energy

If you asked me, "Andrii, what is the single most important thing for being able to work at peak performance?" I would certainly say, "Having enough sleep because there are no time management techniques that can compensate for productivity lost due to fatigue." A brain just like any mechanism needs regular maintenance and in order to be able to function at full capacity during the day the body needs to repair tired neurotransmitters in your brain during the night. The night sleep charges your internal battery with energy necessary to be productive the next day. The average person needs between 7 and 9 hours of sleep, however according to a national survey the average American gets about 6.7 hours of sleep which means that sleep deprivation is a major problem because millions of people don't have enough sleep at night.

Lack of sleep leads to reduced brain performance including thinking, memorizing and learning abilities. Sleep deprivation may cause irritation, inability to focus, lower resistance to stress, depressive feelings and lack of energy. Also, if you haven't spent enough hours in bed your body will have a decreased level of the hormone responsible for appetite regulation, leptin. This decrease in leptin reduces your resistance to eating large portions of unhealthy food and reduces metabolism, which affects the body's ability to utilize the consumed food. So lack of high-quality sleep makes you worse at thinking, makes you less productive, makes you more depressed, makes you overweight and also makes you less energetic. Perhaps one of the most effective ways to increase your level of energy if you are sleep deprived is to begin sleeping enough hours and make sure that your sleep is of high quality.

There are several things that you can take care of before going to bed to significantly increase the quality of your sleep:

1. Go to bed every day and wake up at the same time (within a 30-minute spread)

When you often change your bedtime, the body experiences stress and a lot of energy is spent for this adjustment. When you go to bed every day at the same time, your body gets used to it and you get more rest and energy from the same number of sleep hours.

2. Create the perfect environment for sleep

The perfect environment for sleep is a completely dark and silent bedroom, with a high-quality mattress, in which the temperature is set optimally for sleeping: between 60 and 67 degrees Fahrenheit. Darkness, silence, optimal room temperature and a good mattress improve quality of sleep, so that you gain more energy.

3. Don't eat or drink before going to bed

If you eat before bedtime your body will spend energy on digestion during the night and the quality of your sleep will suffer. People sleep in 5 phases and in order to get to the latest phases that are most effective for energy replenishment you need to sleep several hours in a row without interruption. If you drink a lot of liquid before going to bed you may wake up at night to go to the bathroom. This will interrupt your sleep and reduce your quality of sleep and as a result you will be less energetic in the morning.

4. Maintain perfect weight

In a study conducted by Deakin University in Australia the level of the stress hormone cortisol was measured among 19 men with healthy weight and 17 overweight men after a meal. The subjects were all asked to eat a meal with the same caloric content and the same amount of protein, fat and carbohydrates. After consuming the meal the men of healthy weight showed a 5% increase in cortisol level, where overweight and obese men experienced a 51% increase in cortisol level. An increased level of cortisol in the body leads to higher blood sugar, lower insulin sensitivity and reduced quality of sleep. Scientists from Johns Hopkins University School of Medicine conducted a study among 77 people who were overweight to find out how weight loss may affect the quality of sleep. They found that a group of people who lost on average 15 pounds during the experiment and reduced their belly fat by 15% improved their sleep quality by 20%. If you are overweight, reaching the perfect weight will not only increase your energy level but also improve your quality of sleep during the night.

5. Exercise regularly and eat healthy food

Exercises and healthy nutrition increase quality and amount of sleep. By regularly exercising and eating nutrient-rich food you will fall asleep faster, the sleep will be deeper, interruptions in sleep will be less likely and you will become more energetic. Exercises and healthy nutrition improve countless aspects of our health and sleep is not an exception.

6. Get light exposure only during the day

Production of melatonin that is essential for our sleep is controlled by light exposure. The brain secretes more melatonin when it is dark, which helps you sleep, and it secretes less melatonin during the daytime or when there is light in the room, which keeps you awake and alert. To get a better night sleep and more energy during the day you need to make your bedroom as dark as possible at night by closing the blinds or curtains and switching off electronic devices. During the day, however, you need to expose yourself to natural light as much as possible by spending more time in sunlight and letting more sunlight into your work area. In a recent study researchers from Northwestern University in Chicago discovered that people who work in offices with windows get on average 173% more white light exposure during the day than workers in offices without windows. As a result workers in offices with windows get on average 46 minutes more sleep per night, are more energetic and happier. On the other hand employees in offices without windows report poorer sleep quality and a lower level of energy and life satisfaction. The production of melatonin is heavily affected by light exposure and if most of the time when you sleep it is dark outside and most of the time when you are awake it is sunny outside and you have access to windows, then your sleep quality and level of energy will significantly increase. When part of the time that you sleep it's bright outside, for example in the morning hours, you might find a thick curtain very helpful.

Sleep is the time when our energy is restored and if you make sure that you sleep enough hours and your sleep is of high quality you will become significantly more energetic and as a result productive and happy.

Too-healthy people

Most people understand that if you don't exercise, if you regularly eat junk food, if you are overweight it will hurt your health. Very few people understand that you can hurt yourself by being "too healthy" although it may require significant effort.

Some people realize that being overweight is unhealthy and think: "Well the less I weigh the better I look and the healthier I am." At the beginning when they lose weight their health improves, peaking when they reach the perfect weight for their height and bodily constitution. After that if they significantly reduce their weight below their perfect weight point they become underweight and get anorexia or bulimia. Being significantly underweight is as dangerous for health and energy as being significantly overweight, so your goal shouldn't be always reducing weight, but it should be reaching your perfect weight and then maintaining it for the rest of your life.

Some people realize that alkaline food such as broccoli, spinach or avocado is considered healthy, and acid food is unhealthy. They think: "So if I want to be healthy I will just eat broccoli, spinach or avocado." This decision will hurt their health significantly because our body needs the blood pH balance to be in the range 7.35 to 7.45 and if you eat just alkaline food the pH will be below 7.35. Most people who eat too much unhealthy food have a pH balance below 7.35, however if you eat only extremely healthy food and nothing else you may reach a pH level that is higher than 7.45 and it also will be unhealthy. If about 60% of your food is alkaline and 40% is acid, it would be perfect for your health because pH will be in its perfect range of 7.35 to 7.45. If instead of 60% of alkaline food, you eat 80% or 100% of alkaline food, it is as dangerous for the body as only eating hamburgers and sweets.

Some people realize that exercising is good for their health and think: "I want to be as healthy as I can, so I will exercise as much as possible." Such people may hurt their health significantly but from a different angle than people with a sedentary lifestyle. For example if instead of jogging for one hour you decided to run 10 marathons in a row, if instead of exercising for recreational purposes you become a professional athlete, you may wear out your body quickly and become even more unhealthy than a person who never exercised in his or her life.

The point here is that for weight, nutrition and exercising there is a perfect spot after which increased effort will diminish the positive results. With weight loss you need to reach your perfect weight and stop decreasing it further. With exercises you need to make them part of your life but don't become "too healthy" and destroy your body through inhumane loads. With food make your diet healthy but don't get crazy about eating only alkaline food as you will stop getting important nutrients from acid food and your pH balance will get outside a healthy range. The best thing that you can do for your life is leading a healthy lifestyle, however think twice before becoming "too healthy." In everything you do there is a perfect spot that will maximize your health and energy, after which additional effort to become even healthier will bring negative results.

Vacation and rest

There are two types of fatigue: local fatigue and accumulated fatigue. Local fatigue can be fixed by a short 5 or 15 minute break, however to fix accumulated fatigue you need either a day off at the end of the week or a 1 week vacation that is recommended to take every 3 months. The majority of people in companies around the world have 2 days off each weekend and 4 weeks of vacation per year. Many years ago companies started giving workers this time off not because they wanted to look nice, but because they had calculated that if people get all this time to relax they will be more productive. Whether you are an employee or an entrepreneur, use this time to fix your accumulated fatigue and with a high level of energy you will be able to complete more high-impact tasks than people who don't rest and fight with their sleepiness and lack of concentration.

Several years ago I worked an entire year without vacation and experienced fatigue and low productivity almost every day. I kept saying to my wife, "I urgently need a vacation. I urgently need a vacation, I urgently need a vacation." Although the project I was working on was extremely important and I didn't want to stop working on it I realized, "My productivity is so low now and fatigue so high that if I don't take vacation right now it may take eternity to finish what I am working on." My wife and I went to Egypt for a 1 week vacation and after a shuttle brought us to the hotel and I plugged my notebook into the outlet I shouted, "What? There is no Internet!" For the entire week I didn't think about work. I was tanning, swimming, walking, exercising and sleeping. After we returned home from vacation I experienced a huge burst of energy and felt that I could do more in one day than I used to do during the entire week prior to vacation.

Often people experience laziness because they are mentally and physically exhausted and if you recharge yourself during a weekend you will have much more energy during the days when you need to make progress on the way to your goals. Remember that watching TV, surfing social networks, eating sweets or drinking alcohol are NOT effective ways to rest. During the weekend a walk in a park, a workout, a meeting with friends or going to a theater helps to take your mind away from tasks that you deal with during a work week.

Perhaps the best way to spend a vacation for recharging is to go as far away from your house as possible to travel, to rest at a seaside resort or to go to the mountains. After a vacation, for the next 3 months you will have a lot of life energy for intensive work.

Whether you rest at the end of the work day, during a weekend or during a vacation, remember that one of the most effective ways to recharge is to spend time actively outside and interact with nature. Being exposed to sunlight releases endorphins and serotonin in your body which improves your mood. Also exposure to sunlight suppresses release of melatonin which improves your energy during the day and quality of sleep during the night. When you spend time in nature, for example in a forest, in a park or at the beach, you calm down, recover from stress and your brain rests. Exercise that goes hand-in-hand with spending time in nature such as walking, biking or swimming boosts production of endorphins that make you feel happy and energetic. When you spend time in nature the body and mind restore effectively and you are charged with energy as if you were connected to an energy outlet designed for humans.

Each professional athlete knows that one of the most important ways to restore energy is to be able to rest effectively, because if you do, you will be able to train effectively. The same is true for everyone, if you rest effectively, you will have significantly more energy for your life and as a result you will be happier. Resting effectively is at least as important as your work.

Positive lifestyle

RELOCAte to a high-performance state

One day, while a student at the University of Michigan, I went to a bar with my friends and several alumni to celebrate the end of the school year. After we ordered drinks and started a conversation, I said something funny and everybody laughed. I told another joke and everybody laughed, again. That afternoon the best comedians would have envied my ability to tell jokes on the spot, and for about 2 hours everyone was laughing really hard. I often struggle to come up with a great joke, but that afternoon I couldn't stop the flow of amazing jokes coming to my mind.

Do you remember a time when you were significantly more productive than usual? Researchers who model and replicate behavior of successful people found that the state we are in has a huge effect on our ability to work productively and we are most effective in a high-performance state.

In a high-performance state, people are relaxed, excited, lively, open and confident. The opposite is also true. If you become relaxed, excited, lively, open and confident simultaneously, you will get into the high-performance state and become dramatically more effective at whatever you do.

When actors play a role and want to convey a particular emotion of the character, they need to evoke it in themselves. They remember a situation from life when they felt this emotion clearly, relive it in their imagination and very soon begin to feel the emotion. This technique from the world of acting will help you with getting into a high-performance state.

To get into a high-performance state, you need to become simultaneously relaxed, excited, lively, open and confident. When these 5 states are combined, their individual effects on performance increase many times.

Relaxed

Relax all the muscles in your body completely except for the ones you need to stay upright. First, flex all your muscles and then quickly relax them. Relax all the muscles from your head to your feet. Pay attention to your breathing. Notice that each time you breathe and exhale, your body relaxes more and more until you are fully relaxed.

Excited

Remember a time in your life when you were really excited and relive this situation in your mind. Feel the excitement again. You are spontaneous and open for new opportunities and behaviors. Feel yourself excited and secure because your task at hand is just a game.

Lively

Become energetic. Feel the power within you and your readiness to do something. To become energetic, jump, dance, do physical exercise or just remember how it felt when you did something active. If you imagine it clearly enough, your nervous system won't notice any difference. Remember, however, that you need to build up your energy while staying completely relaxed. As soon as you notice tension – relax yourself. It might seem impossible to be lively and relaxed simultaneously, but it is easy. It's an amazing feeling of outside calmness and internal readiness.

Open

Remember a time when you were ready to accept anything that the world has to offer. You don't know what will happen in the next moment, but it is not important because you are ready to accept anything. Build up a feeling of openness until you can clearly feel it.

Confident

Recall a situation from your life when you felt absolutely confident in yourself. Maybe you said or did something you were 100% sure about. Relive it as clearly as you can and feel what you felt at that time. While building up a feeling of confidence, remain open, lively, excited and relaxed.

Again

Repeat again everything mentioned above! Every time you increase the intensity of each feeling, make sure you stay simultaneously relaxed, excited, lively, open and confident. Go through this list several times and very soon you will get into a high-productivity state.

The high-productivity state will help you to become significantly more effective in whatever you do and everything will work out. I highly recommend getting into this state when you have an important meeting, need to prepare a speech, need to generate creative ideas, or simply work on an important project. RELOCAte is a very powerful technique that will boost your energy level and will make you more successful. You always are in a high-performance state when you play a favorite game and you are never in a high-performance state when you are serious and have a straight face. To be significantly more productive and to stay in a high-performance state for a long time, have an attitude that what you do is an interesting game rather than serious work.

Positive attitude

What if you could be in a high-performance state most of the time? If you are, you will experience more fun from your life and you will be significantly more productive and successful. Increasing the amount of time that you are in a high-performance state will give you a magic power with which you will be able to achieve anything.

When you are angry, stressed, scared or depressed your energy level significantly lowers and it seems that you can't accomplish even simple tasks. When you are in a good mood, when you are excited, when you feel drive, your energy level increases and the biggest breakthroughs in life happen. The secret of staying in a high-performance state long term is increasing the amount of positive emotions that you experience and decreasing the amount of negative emotions that you experience within a day. Remember that emotions that you experience today will create your tomorrow, and emotions that you experience tomorrow will create your day after tomorrow. To be highly productive you need to be excited about your future and be in a good mood most of the time, and for this you need to increase the amount of positive thoughts and decrease the amount of negative thoughts that cross your mind within a day.

In an experiment conducted by researchers from the University of Minnesota, 4-year-old children were asked to think for 30 seconds a positive thought, a neutral thought or a negative thought before participating in a task that involved solving logical problems. Children who had a positive thought completed a task more than two times faster and with fewer mistakes than children who thought a negative thought. If just one thought had such a significant impact on children's performance, imagine how much an adult's performance can be affected by hundreds of thoughts that cross his or her mind every day.

Many years ago an old Cherokee Native American told his grandson: "Every day a battle between two wolves happens in your head. One wolf is negativity: anger, stress, sadness, fear, hate, shame, guilt, embarrassment, disgust, contempt. Another wolf is positivity: amusement, inspiration, interest, drive, hope, pride, amusement, awe and love." The grandson thought for a moment and asked: "And which wolf wins?" The grandfather looked at his grandson and said: "The one you feed." Positive thoughts that you feed into your brain give you energy, negative thoughts suck energy out of you.

The biggest breakthroughs happen when you are in a good mood and have fun doing what you do. Don't let yourself become serious and postpone being happy for the future. You need to get used to being in a good mood, to pumping yourself with positive emotions, and you will be in a high-performance state most of the time. When children are playing their favorite games they are excited, they are relaxed, they are lively, they are open, they are confident, and they are in a high-performance state. If your attitude toward work is that it is an interesting game, if your attitude to life is that it is an exciting adventure, you will become more productive, more successful, and more energetic.

A sunny disposition is worth more than fortune. Young people should know that it can be cultivated; that the mind like the body can be moved from the shade into sunshine. — Andrew Carnegie

Take control over negative thoughts

All events in your life are neutral and only your interpretation can make your life either a flourishing garden or a terrible hell. Your negative reaction to negative events gives your mind an impulse that attracts even more negative events in future. Here are the main causes of energy leakage that may make you less active, less productive and less happy:

1. Quarrels

Even if you are a winner in an argument you will lose a lot of energy. Try to avoid conflicts where you can, especially with friends and family. Even more dangerous than a quarrel are negative thoughts that will regularly come to your head when you remember it.

2. Complaints

For example: "I wasn't born in a wealthy family," "I am not lucky," "I don't have enough money," "People don't value me," "I didn't achieve much by 30," "There is no justice in the world," "Somebody didn't do what was promised." Complaints suck life energy out of you and make your life even worse in future.

3. Being stuck in negative thoughts

Thinking about debts that you need to pay off or people who owe money to you, blaming yourself and others, thinking about potential failure, feeling resentment for your past actions, fearing something undesirable will happen. Being stuck in negative thoughts can create numerous negative emotions for you every day and as a result what you fear most, what you don't like most, what you hate most will increase in your life.

To reduce the amount of negative thoughts that cross your mind firstly remove sources of negative thoughts and secondly change your attitude to negative events.

You might think: "How can I remove sources of negative thoughts?" There are multiple ways to do so. If you have to deal with people who regularly create negative emotions in you, reduce communication with them as much as possible. Forgive all people who did anything bad to you, to get rid of negative thoughts that destroy you from within. Pay off all your debts and avoid lending money to other people unless you are ready to give it as a gift. Stop comparing yourself to other people as there will be always someone smarter, richer, luckier, with a bigger house, with a better body, and compete only with yourself.

You might think: "How can I change my attitude about negative events?" You need to understand that all failures that you experience are 100% positive because they teach you a valuable lesson, they help you to make progress and they open new opportunities even if you don't understand them yet. Instead of letting the failure pass through you and letting negative thoughts bring harm to your life, ask yourself: "What positive can I get out of this failure?" To be happy – you need to be glad for your failures and consider them as an interesting challenge or a valuable experience that is an essential part of your journey to the life of your dreams.

When you face a problem instead of thinking negative thoughts ask yourself: "How can I solve this problem?" After that take massive actions to resolve the problem in the best possible way. If you succeed you will experience positive emotions. If you fail and you can honestly say: "I did everything that depended on me, there is nothing else I could do," congratulate yourself for doing great work. If a problem came to your life, instead of regretting what already happened create an action plan that will allow you to resolve it. If the reason for a failure was external circumstances that you didn't have any control over, avoid beating yourself up and move on. Change your focus from negative thoughts to taking action and trying to do best what is under your control.

Negative thoughts suck energy out of you and in order to increase your energy level you need to decrease their amount. There are three effective ways to reduce the amount of negative thoughts coming to your head: eliminate sources of negative thoughts, consider failures as valuable lessons and turn problems into actions. Negative thoughts are part of life and no matter what you do, you will not be able to get rid of them completely, however your goal is just to reduce their amount.

Whether you think you can, or you think you can't – you're right. – Henry Ford

You are going to enjoy all the bullshit you have to deal with as you chase your goals and dreams, because you want to remember them all.

Each and every experience will serve as motivation and provide great memories when you finally make it all happen... – Mark Cuban

The recipe for depression is pessimism meeting failure and then ruminating endlessly about it. – Anonymous

Power of a present moment

In their research Harvard psychologists Matthew Killingsworth and Daniel Gilbert have analyzed the thoughts that come to people's minds throughout the day. They contacted 2,250 volunteers at random intervals through an iPhone application and asked what they were doing at the moment, what they were thinking about and how happy they felt. On average, respondents reported that 46.9% of the time their mind was wandering and they were not thinking about the task at hand. Another interesting finding was that only 4.6% of happiness that people experienced was related to the task that they were doing, and mind-wandering status impacted 10.8% of their happiness. Killingsworth and Gilbert wrote: "A human mind is a wandering mind, and a wandering mind is an unhappy mind. The ability to think about what is not happening is a cognitive achievement that comes at an emotional cost."

When people allow their mind to wander uncontrollably they tend to think negative thoughts about the future or past. For example they might think about bad events that happened in the past or fear bad events that might happen in the future, they might think about a recent quarrel with a friend or an upcoming unpleasant conversation with a colleague, they might blame themselves for what they didn't do well in the past or fear the ambiguity of what may happen to them in the future. All negative thoughts that cross your mind are related either to the past or to the future and if your mind is focused on the present moment then it is protected from negative emotions at least temporarily. Worrying about past or future won't make your life better, but taking care of a present moment certainly would.

 If you regularly remind yourself to focus your attention completely on a present moment your productivity will increase and you will become 10.8% happier. Remember that the best and the most important moment in your life is right now. Our life consists of years, years consist of months, months consist of days and days consist of moments. If you try to get maximum results from the present moment, if you try to get maximum joy from the present moment, if you try to get maximum happiness from the present moment, and after that do the same with the next moment, then your entire life will be successful, joyful and happy. Returning your mind from time to time to a present moment is a technique that is extremely effective for improving mood, energy level, and quality of life. Live in a present moment, give the entire you to a present moment, get the maximum of everything from a present moment.

My philosophy is that not only are you responsible for your life but doing the best at this moment puts you in the best place for the next moment. – Oprah Winfrey

Positive filter

At the beginning of his career my father worked in a company where was impressed by his colleague Ludmila, who was around 60 years old at the time. He said to me: "Ludmila is the most positive person I have ever seen. Every time you see her she is in a good mood." One day my father overheard Ludmila being told off by her manager in his office. The manager was in a rage: he was shouting at her, he was swearing at her, and he was hitting a fist on the table. When Ludmila went out of her manager's office and my father saw her she was calm, in a good mood and smiling. He asked: "Ludmila, how do you manage to stay calm and positive after such a terrible conversation?" She said: "Due to my health condition I can't experience stress. My doctor told me that if I experience stress I will die, so I don't have a choice, either I always stay calm and positive and don't react to negative events, or I will die." That day my father was startled by her answer and decided consciously to always be positive himself. If Ludmila is the most positive person that my father has ever seen in his life, then my father is the most positive person that I have seen in my life. No matter what negative happens to him, no matter what problems he has, no matter what difficulties he goes through, he is always positive, in a good mood and smiling.

By default people have a negative filter and if they have 99% of positive things in their life and 1% of negative things they tend to focus on this 1% of negative things and this draws even more negative things to their lives. If you want to become more positive, energetic and happy you need to make a conscious decision to look at the world through a positive filter and focus your attention on the 99% of things that are good in your life. Let's discuss three extremely effective techniques that will allow you to tune your positive filter.

Gratitude technique

Develop a habit of telling yourself every morning 5 things that are great in your life and you are grateful for. These 5 things shouldn't necessarily be big or significant. For example: "The sun is shining. Awesome!" "I have a computer. Awesome!" "I have two legs and two hands. Awesome!" "I exercised yesterday. Awesome!" "I have a goal that I am passionate about. Awesome!" "I have a friend. Awesome!" "I can speak. Awesome!" "I am alive. Awesome!" Try to use different things every time to make your brain get used to the idea that there are many things it can be grateful for.

The gratitude technique is very effective because it helps you to notice good things that are present in your life, tunes your positivity filter and makes your life better. Once you have practiced the gratitude technique long enough, you will be looking at the same world around you however through positive lenses and will notice significantly more positive things than before. As a result, the amount of positive thoughts that cross your mind will increase. Tune your internal radio on a positivity wave and your brain, out of millions of different thoughts that can potentially come to your head, will focus more on positive ones. If you begin each day being glad for what is already great in your life, you will not only have a better mood, you will not only be happier but you will also draw even more positive things to your life. When you appreciate what you already have, you give your brain a task: "Bring more similar positive things to my life. I appreciate them." And with such a task your brain will work 24/7 on attracting positive events to your life and you will get into a never-ending flow of positive events. Learn how to be happy about your life even without a significant reason and your life quality will significantly improve.

People often think that happiness is conditional: "If I get accepted to Harvard then I will become happy." "If I get promoted then I will be happy." "When I create a successful business, then I will be happy." "When I get married then I will be happy." However happiness works vice versa. You don't achieve goals and because of that you are happy, but you are happy and because of that you achieve your goals. When you are in a positive mood you are in a high-performance state. Your motivation, productivity and energy increase manifold and they help you to get to any goals significantly faster. Learn how to be grateful for what you already have in your life, be happy right now and this will attract even more awesome things to your life.

Anticipate good events

Professor Lee Berk of Loma Linda University conducted a study in which he researched how anticipation of positive events affects our body. In an experiment a first group of people was told that they were going to watch a humorous video and a second group of people (a control group) was told simply to wait. The blood drawn from experimental subjects just before they watched the video had 27% more endorphins than the control group. This study confirms that anticipation of positive events improves mood and makes people feel happier. Having positive events in future that you can anticipate is one of the most effective techniques for raising your energy level. You might think: "What positive can I anticipate?"

Firstly, put positive events on your calendar that you know will bring you joy and that you can anticipate. For example: Schedule your next vacation, schedule visiting a theater or a cinema, schedule meeting with friends or schedule an interesting experience. The anticipation of a positive event will increase the amount of endorphins in your blood, it will make you think positive thoughts about this event and it will raise your mood. In fact anticipating a positive event often brings more joy than the event itself. If you schedule a vacation that will happen a month from now, anticipation of this event will bring you joy and positive thoughts the entire month, after that the vacation itself will bring you joy and positive thoughts, and after that remembering the vacation will bring you joy and positive thoughts. To be happy and energetic you need to have positive events to anticipate, so develop a habit of scheduling positive events in your life and the more the better.

Secondly, visualize regularly the moment when your big goal is achieved. Positive thoughts about achieving your short-term and long-term goals motivate you to take action, which not only helps to create ideas, but also makes you anticipate these positive events and as a result raises endorphins in your blood, your mood and energy.

Many studies have confirmed that experiences bring significantly more positive emotions than physical possessions so to become emotionally rich you need to collect experiences rather than things. Not only experiences themselves bring positive emotions but also anticipation of these experiences and later remembering these experiences. To be happy and emotionally rich you need to pump your life with positive experiences. You can schedule pleasurable events such as attending a concert, meeting with interesting people, participating in a sports competition, traveling to a foreign country or doing what you have never done before. Also you can set goals and a process of achieving them will move you from one positive experience to another. Life is an interesting adventure novel and you are the author.

Celebrate success

When I was 9 I attended both a dancing school and a karate school. At a dancing school I enjoyed the lessons, worked hard and made a lot of progress. At karate school I couldn't wait for the lesson to end, was lazy and didn't make any progress. When I thought: "Why is my behavior was so different?" I realized that although I was very awkward in both places, in karate school I was only criticized for what I did wrong, but in dancing school I received a lot of positive comments about what I did well and less comments about what I could improve.

In a study conducted by the University of Michigan Business School, the performance of many corporate teams was compared to the frequency of praise and criticism given within the workplace. It turned out that the best performing team had a praise to criticism ratio of above 5 and the lowest performing teams had a ratio lower than 0.35. You can apply this principle to your personal life. In order to increase your self-esteem, motivation and productivity you need to increase the amount of times when you appreciate what you already did well.

In the evening evaluate what tasks you managed to accomplish within a day, how much progress you made toward a goal and celebrate small intermediate successes that you experienced. Say to yourself: "I succeed and this is normal." When you focus attention on your successes that you experience every day, you generate positive thoughts in your head and train your brain that succeeding is normal for you. Your self-esteem will increase, your mood will increase, your motivation to succeed even more will increase and as a result you will become more energetic and happy. Success is a huge source of energy and in addition to working towards future success, you need to recognize success that you have every day no matter how small it is. If before going to bed you recognize what success you made within a day, your mind will get used to finishing each day successfully and will be excited to wake up in the morning and to experience even more success. Success breeds success, success breeds positive thoughts, success breeds happiness. What is appreciated increases in size, if you are glad for the success that you already have, the amount of success and positive events in your life will increase.

When you begin looking at the world with a positive attitude, good things begin to get attracted to you and your life indeed becomes awesome. When you are positive, you remain in a high-performance state most of the time and as a result your productivity increases manifold. It's important to make a conscious decision to be positive because the more positive energy there is in your internal accumulator, the easier it will be to achieve goals and the higher your average energy level will be. Be grateful for good things that are already present in your life, anticipate good things that will happen to you in future, and appreciate success that you have achieved within a day.

Belief creates the actual fact. – William James

For years I've been advocating the power and pleasure of being grateful. I kept a gratitude journal for a full decade without fail—and urged you all to do the same. – Oprah Winfrey

Rule of 100 smiles

Let's return to my meeting at a restaurant with Jason, the billionaire and serial entrepreneur that you read about at the beginning of the book. After a waiter took our orders Jason shared with me a tip that has dramatically affected the amount of energy that I have during the day.

Jason sipped tea, smiled and said: "Many years ago I was divorced from my wife and my business went bankrupt within the same year. I was broken, I was depressed and I didn't want to do anything. From a friend of a friend of a friend I learned about a monastery in Tibet to which people with depression come from all over the world and get healed with the help of a smile.

"When I arrived at the monastery the head monk said: 'In our monastery all monks are constantly smiling and you have to do the same. Our monks will be watching you and if someone notices you at least once not smiling you will have to spend with us one more day. When you manage to spend the entire day with a smile on a face your healing will be over.'

"At first I thought that this task was easy, however it took me two weeks to live an entire day with a smile on my face. These two weeks were the happiest time in my life, I met many interesting people, I learned a lot about philosophy of life from the monks, and most importantly I began feeling myself happier than ever before. The head monk said: 'Jason, your first stage of healing is finished. You learned how to smile when everybody around you is smiling. Now you need to return to your everyday life and learn how to smile when you are the only one smiling.'

"Andrii, when you smile three hormones of happiness are released to your body: endorphins, dopamine and serotonin. These hormones make you feel motivated, confident and happy. When people feel great they smile, however the opposite is also true, when they smile they feel great. The way to have more positive energy is to increase the amount of smiles in your life. The formula of happiness is: 'Number of smiles minus number of frowns.'

"By statistics unhappy people smile 5 times per day, average people smile 20 times per day, happy people smile 50 times per day and children smile 400 times per day. For many years I have been following a rule of 100 smiles which says that you have to smile 100 times per day and this significantly improved my level of energy and happiness. It doesn't matter how you smile: You can smile while talking to friends. You can smile while watching funny videos. You can smile at people who you pass by on the street. You can smile remembering a positive event from the past. You can smile being glad for your success. You can make a fake smile. The most important thing is to make sure that you smile at least 100 times per day."

There is little success where there is little laughter. — Andrew Carnegie

Sometimes your joy is the source of your smile, but sometimes your smile can be the source of your joy. — Thich Nhat Hanh

We shall never know all the good that a simple smile can do. — Mother Teresa

Magic of passion

Sail on passion

Between 1960 and 1980 a psychologist, Dr. Srully Blotnick, conducted research based on 1,500 business school graduates. He grouped them into two categories. Category A said they would pursue money first and would do what they are passionate about later in life. This category consisted of 1,245 people which represented 83% of all graduates. Category B said that they would focus on their passion and trust that money would follow. This category consisted of 255 people, which represented 17% of all graduates. Twenty years later there were 101 millionaires out of the original group of 1,500 people. What startled Blotnick was that only 1 millionaire was from Category A (follow the money) and 100 millionaires were from Category B (follow your passion). If you were one of the graduates in this study who consciously decided to build life around what you are passionate about, your chances for becoming a millionaire would be 488 times higher than if you built your life around a desire to become rich.

Perhaps the most effective way to increase your energy level is doing work that you are passionate about. On the way to your goals you can get energy only from two sources: willpower and passion. With willpower you can do work that you don't particularly like, however this source of energy is limited and can be quickly depleted. Passion is an unlimited source of energy, and if you rely on it, you will be able to make significantly faster progress towards your goals. If you are passionate about your work you will have more positive emotions, a higher level of energy, a better mood and as a result will become significantly happier. Successful people always do what they love, because doing what you love is much more powerful fuel on the way to a goal than willpower.

Imagine a time when you were a child playing a favorite game. The time passed fast, you were enthusiastic and felt filled. Imagine a time when you were a child and had to do a household chore or study your least favorite subject. The time passed slowly, you were bored and felt empty. When children select what to do, they choose based on their feelings, however when adults select what to do they make a selection based on logic. Children think: "I would rather play a game than do a household chore because playing makes me happy and doing household chores or learning my least favorite subject makes me unhappy." Adults think: "I will become a programmer because it is prestigious. I need to go to Harvard because my parents will be proud of me. I will work for company X because the salary is excellent." When people select what to do based on logic the time passes slowly at work, they are bored and feel empty. They have many logical reasons why they made the right career choice, however without passion it's impossible to succeed or be happy.

The only way to succeed in your work is to be passionate about it. The only way to identify what you are passionate about is to listen to your internal feeling of emptiness or fullness. If you have a hypothesis of what your vocation is, imagine yourself doing this work, turn off the logic and notice how you feel inside. If you feel excited and work is filling you with energy, then this is your vocation. If you feel bored and need to apply willpower, then this work is anything but your vocation. You can lie to your head, but you can't lie to your body. Listening to your body is significantly more reliable than listening to your head when selecting a vocation. If you do not feel passionate about something, you will never find enough motivation to be great at it. One of the most important tasks in life is to figure out what you are passionate about and then focus your time, mind and energy to do this work very well.

Passion is when you are excited to wake up every day to make progress in your favorite work. Passion is when you are smiling a lot, when you have fun doing your work, and when you feel that you occupy exactly the place in the world that you were created for. Passion is when your goals are inspiring you, when you are obsessed about them, and when making progress towards them makes you as excited as a kid receiving a Christmas present. Passion is when you are constantly thinking about your work in the morning, during the day and before going to bed. Passion is when you would be happy to do your work on Sunday even if you weren't paid for it. Everybody has a mission and if you follow your mission then everything begins to work out, you become lucky, the necessary resources are easily attracted, it seems that you are stroking along the current and get into a flow of positive events. If you decide that the mission doesn't matter and you logically select a job that isn't your passion – you lack energy, your effort brings little results and it seems that you are hitting your head at the imaginary wall.

There are no lazy people – there are only people who are not passionate about their work. Acting out of character or trying to live your neighbor's life depletes willpower and sucks energy out of you. Energy comes only when you are able to apply your unique talents and have courage to do the work that you are passionate about. The most important decision that you can ever make is to refuse to be driven by expectations of other people, and instead follow your vocation and do the work that fills your body with energy and heart with joy.

You know you are on the road to success if you would do your job, and not be paid for it. — Oprah Winfrey

I always tell myself that we are born here not to work, but to enjoy life. We are here to make things better for one another, and not to work. If you are spending your whole life working, you will certainly regret it. — Jack Ma

The biggest mistake people make in life is not trying to make a living at doing what they most enjoy. — Malcolm Forbes

Choose a job you love, and you will never have to work a day in your life — Confucius

More than any other element, fun is the secret of Virgin's success. — Richard Branson

Without passion you don't have energy, without energy you have nothing. — Donald Trump

Nothing great has ever been accomplished without enthusiasm. — Ralph Waldo Emerson

Questions for internal conversation

The only person who can identify what you are passionate about is you. Below is a list of questions thinking about which will inspire your internal dialogue that will make clearer what your true vocation is. Ask yourself each of the 25 questions below, think for at least 5 minutes before moving to the next one and write down ideas that come to your head. After this exercise when you have ideas written down they will either make crystal clear for you what you are passionate about or will make you closer to figuring it out. Remember that just reading these questions won't bring you any value, however thinking about them and later answering them will make you understand yourself better and might help to answer the most important question in your life: "What is my vocation?" Now devote the necessary time to conversation with your inner self and answer each of the questions below.

1) What would you do if you had $1 billion?

2) How would you know that you live a passionate life?

3) What things do you enjoy doing, give you satisfaction, fill you with energy and make you really excited and happy?

4) What is your personality?

5) What comes easy to you?

6) What are or where your interests?

7) What do you REALLY want?

8) What is your inner voice telling you?

9) What makes your blood boil?

10) When were you in a high-performance state?

11) If you were guaranteed success, what would you do?

12) In the future, when you're already living a passionate life, what advice would you give to the present you?

13) What activities give meaning and purpose to your life?

14) What do you most often daydream about?

15) What do you really want to be, have and do?

16) What raises your self-esteem, gives you fulfillment and makes you feel important?

17) What do you want to be famous for?

18) What would you do if you had a magic wand?

19) If you could do just one thing all day long what would it be?

20) What work would you do on Sunday even if you weren't paid for it?

21) What ideas excite you the most and what people would you like to surround yourself with?

22) Who are your heroes that you want to resemble in something?

23) In what work could you fully realize your potential?

24) What can you do to make the biggest contribution to the world?

25) What can you do for hours and not notice how the time passed?

Asking these questions from time to time will help you to make sure that you are doing the work that you were created for and that you clearly understand what you are passionate about. If you still don't know what you are passionate about, don't worry, continue trying different experiences in life and asking these questions. Figuring out your vocation and devoting your entire life to it is one of the most important things in life. If you give yourself a task to clarify what you are passionate about, sooner or later you will know who you are and what you should be doing with full clarity.

The passion test

When you have found your vocation, the work fills you with energy and makes you experience positive emotions regularly. You can lie to your head however you can't lie to your body, so when selecting a vocation you will find very handy a passion test. Below we will discuss 3 potential applications of this test.

Firstly, every day listen to your internal feelings and ask yourself: "Am I doing the right thing? Does what I am doing fill me or empty me?" The answer to this question will give you a hint if you should do more of it or less of it. To become successful you need to increase the amount of peak moments in your life when you feel the most energetic, the most proud of yourself and the happiest. By remembering which activities have generated peak moments in your past and which activities generate peak moments in your present, you can come to understand what your vocation is and what work you are passionate about. As self-made billionaire Oleg Boyko said: "Psychology is the most important thing. Emotions and again emotions – through them any heights are achieved."

Secondly, if you have a hypothesis of what you might be passionate about, imagine that you are having this experience for many years. For a few minutes try to make this potential life as real as possible in your head and think what you see, what you hear, what you smell. Now notice how your body responds: Does this experience make you excited and filled or does it make you bored and empty? If you feel positive emotions inside while thinking about this experience then it is your vocation, if you don't then most probably it is something that you convinced yourself logically might be a good career choice but will in fact make your life miserable.

Finally in addition to imagining doing an activity from the hypothesis for a few minutes, try to immerse yourself in this experience in real life for a few hours. For example if you have a hypothesis that being a programmer is your vocation try to read about it, try to code for some time, try to attend a programming community meeting, try to talk to a person who has been a programmer for many years. After this, notice your internal feeling and see if this experience is making you happy and filled or bored and empty. You might think: "Well, I didn't feel anything at all. I neither felt bad or good." In this case it's not your vocation, because if you are doing work you are passionate about even thinking about it makes your body respond and experience positive emotions. When you choose a vocation it's the same as when you choose a spouse — you aren't finding a logical reason why he or she is the right choice, you simply know because your body experiences positive emotions being close to this person.

If you have found your vocation you are more productive in your daily work, you experience more happy moments, and you have more energy. Without passion you have to rely only on willpower and this source of energy is limited, is quickly depleted and won't allow you to be successful. To identify what you are passionate about, you need to do just two things. Firstly set a task to regularly think about what your vocation is. And secondly listen to your body and how it responds to various activities. Knowing crystal clear your vocation is one of the most important steps towards an energetic, fulfilled and happy life. All people have a vocation and if you set a goal for yourself to identify what your vocation is, you will certainly find an answer. Take into account that with time what you are passionate about may change and you need to look at your life and ask from time to time: "What am I passionate about?"

Find your talents

My friend Julia wanted to have children and when the doctor said: "Congratulations! You are going to have twins," she and her husband were in seventh heaven. When her sons Mark and Vlad turned 7, Julia signed them up for singing and acrobatics classes. Julia said to me during our conversation over a cup of coffee: "After a year I began realizing how different my children are. Mark enjoyed singing classes, had the best progress in the group and received praise from his teacher. Vlad hated singing classes and didn't make any progress no matter how much effort he applied. With acrobatics classes the situation was completely the opposite. Vlad enjoyed acrobatics classes, had the best progress in the group and received praise from his teacher. Mark hated acrobatics classes and his movements were very awkward no matter how much effort he applied." Julia sighed and added: "One day Mark and Vlad came to me and said: 'Mom, we want to attend more classes we enjoy and stop attending classes we aren't good at.' And I did just what they asked. Every year I noticed how much progress my children made in their areas of interest and how correct this decision has been. Mark started writing his own songs, attended TV show castings and by the age of 20 is already a famous singer. Vlad on the other hand started winning sports competitions and by the age of 20 is performing in one of the most famous circuses in the world. Both my children are happy, successful and well-paid although their talents are completely different."

Remember that at the beginning of the book we defined happiness as an emotion of progress towards a desirable goal.

The formula of progress is the following: Progress towards the goal = (size of your talent) * (amount of effort applied). You can affect the amount of effort that you apply, but the amount of talent that you have in each particular area is fixed. As a result, to become happier you need to make more progress, and to make more progress you need to build your career around your strongest talent.

If you do work that you are talented for, you make significantly more progress with the same amount of effort, you are more successful, you experience more positive emotions, you have higher self-esteem, you are more productive, you are more energetic, and you are happier. Successful people build careers around their core talents and when they see an interesting opportunity that doesn't utilize their core talents they skip it, because they know that long term they won't be able to create much value for the world without using their competitive advantage. If you want to raise your level of energy and happiness, first figure out what your core talents are and then figure out how to apply them on a daily basis. By the way, in the majority of cases the work that you are talented for coincides with the work that you are passionate about.

How to identify talents

All people are talented however everyone has won different talents in a birth lottery. You might not be a genius but you are certainly stronger in certain areas than in others. You need to clearly understand what your strengths are, because if you build your life around them your life will be more successful and happy.

Firstly ask yourself the following questions and write down ideas that come to your head. The internal dialogue encouraged by these questions will allow you to understand yourself better.

1) What are my talents?

2) What do I do especially well that is difficult for other people?

3) If I could do only one activity all day long, what would allow me to bring the most value for society?

4) What activity do I get most compliments from others for?

5) What did I do well in childhood?

6) What I am genius at?

Now evaluate each of the talents that you have written down on a scale from 0 to 100 where 0 means no talent at all and 100 means the most talented person in the world. Those talents that get the highest score are your core talents. The more you utilize them on a daily basis, the bigger progress you will be able to make in your work, the more your body will be filled with energy, and the more your life will be filled with positive emotions.

Understand who you are

Try taking a Myers-Briggs test to identify which of 16 different personality types you are. After that read a brochure about your personality type to learn what are your strengths, what are your weaknesses, how you behave in different situations, what professions are most suitable for you. After reading this information you might think: "Wow. How accurately the book describes who I am." You will not learn anything that you didn't know before about yourself but will realize that being who you are is normal. You and millions of other people with your personality type have certain strengths and weaknesses.

In the past you might have been blamed by yourself or others because of being weak in certain areas, however being weak is normal. Everybody is weak in certain areas and strong in others and people who have a different personality type than yours may be strong in your weak areas and weak in your strong areas.

To be happy and successful you need to figure out what your talents are and focus your time strengthening them even further and applying them. The biggest progress is made when you focus your attention entirely on your strengths and do what you can do best. Ignore your weaknesses and let people who are strong in areas where you are weak do the job that they can do best.

Accept yourself for who you are, don't attempt to live somebody else's life and remember that suffering by doing what comes difficult to you isn't necessary. The most successful people in the world can't do everything – they have only mastered one or two things and do them extraordinary well.

There is nothing more satisfying than being loved for who you are and nothing more painful than being loved for who you're not but pretending to be. – Neil Pasricha

To find out what one is fitted to do, and to secure an opportunity to do it is the key to happiness – John Dewey

Morning energy ritual

There are certain techniques that don't take much time to do but can help you to feel energetic right after waking up. Below you can find 3 things that can make the beginning of your day more pleasurable and successful.

1. Do a 5-minute morning exercise

When people open their eyes it may take up to an hour to completely wake up and feel energetic. A morning exercise allows you to save time and feel awake and energetic right away. Morning exercise isn't a substitute for your regular exercises but a technique for waking up faster, so it shouldn't take longer than 5 minutes and shouldn't be strenuous. One of the most effective morning exercises that was tested on me and my students is a routine called Radio Taiso that is very popular in Japan and that you can easily find on YouTube. Besides Radio Taiso any short morning exercise that you can find will work effectively for waking up.

2. Take a contrast shower

When you take a warm shower in the morning finish it by switching the water temperature to cold and endure the cold shower for a minute. A contrast shower improves blood circulation, burns fat, improves mood and makes you feel energetic.

3. Eat oatmeal with fruits and drink a green tea

Eating oatmeal with fruits is one of the healthiest choices that you can make for breakfast. Oatmeal supplies your body with all necessary nutrients so that you can become energetic. Eating oatmeal leaves you with a feeling of lightness in your stomach which helps to maintain healthy weight and to devote most of the energy that you get to your brain and muscles rather than to the digestive system.

Hot green tea is not only the healthiest drink after water, but it also is excellent for boosting energy. The greatest thing about green tea that it boosts energy without having negative side effects like coffee or soft drinks. You can drink green tea in the morning, at lunch or in the middle of the day to boost energy and to gain numerous health benefits that it provides.

Insane Energy checklist

Before getting to the final chapter of the book let's review most important techniques of the *Insane Energy for Lazy People* system. If you use them in your everyday life you will feel more energetic, your life will have more positive emotions and you will become happier.

1. Set a goal and make progress

Happiness is the emotion of progress towards a desirable goal. Build a list of long-term, average-term and short-term wishes and take massive action to fulfill them. The more progress you have towards the desirable goals the more energy and happiness you will have. The formula of progress is the following: *Progress towards the goal = (size of your talent) * (amount of effort applied)*.

Perhaps the biggest source of energy that you can connect to is passion. When you are passionate about your work, you experience more positive emotions, you are very energetic and productive. If you aren't passionate about your work, you will have to rely on your willpower that is a very limited source of energy that will not allow you to make a significant progress towards your goals and as a result you won't be happy. The only way to be successful is to build your career around work that you are passionate about. By being passionate about your work you can significantly increase *(amount of effort applied)* in the progress formula. You can increase the amount of effort that is applied in a direction of the goal, but the amount of talent that you got in the birth lottery is fixed. To increase *(size of your talent)* in the progress formula figure out what your core talents are and build your career around them.

To be happy you need to make significant progress towards your desirable goals. To make significant progress you need to have talent for and be passionate about your work. *Progress towards the goal = (size of your talent) * (amount of effort applied).* When you are clear about your vocation you will be more energetic, successful and happy.

2. Social connections are energy multiplier

If happiness is an emotion of progress towards a desirable goal, then social connections are a multiplier of happiness that you have. Having good relationships with family members, a spouse and friends significantly increases the amount of positive emotions in life, level of energy and feeling of happiness. Social connections are so powerful that any kind of positive interaction with people will make you feel good: talking to a colleague at work, smiling at a stranger, attending a concert or going to a café.

3. Exercise for energy

Exercise is one of the most effective ways to recover from stress and charge your body with energy. Remember to exercise regularly and include in your training aerobic, muscle and stretching exercises as they all have different benefits. The more energy you lose throughout the day, the more energy your internal battery is charged with, and exercises allow losing more energy within a day.

4. Eat healthy food

Food is an incredibly important source of energy. Make sure to eat healthy food rich with nutrients and you will not only be more energetic, but you will also be able to maintain healthy weight. Remember to add more highly alkaline food to your diet, to remove highly acid food from your diet and to replace all drinks with water and hot green tea.

5. Sleep for energy

During sleep your energy is replenished, so having a high-quality sleep is essential for an active lifestyle. Exercising, eating healthy food and maintaining optimal weight increase quality of sleep. Remember that it's essential to go to bed and wake up every day at the same time and to sleep enough hours. One of the important factors for quality of sleep is light exposure that regulates melatonin production. When you are awake try to expose yourself to natural light as much as possible to feel energetic, and when you sleep make sure that you sleep in a dark room the entire night. When part of the time that you sleep it's bright outside, for example in the morning hours, you might find a thick curtain very helpful.

6. Lose weight

A healthy weight significantly increases the amount of energy that you have and can spend throughout a day. Each lost pound in a direction towards a perfect weight will give you an additional 2% in energy. Also the closer you get to your perfect weight the better your quality of sleep is. Through healthy diet, through exercises and through high-quality sleep you can get to your perfect weight as soon as possible to make your life more energetic, active and happy.

7. Rest on weekends and take vacations

To get rid of accumulated fatigue that can't be fixed by a sleep or a short break, you need to rest on weekends and during a vacation. The best way to recharge your brain is to spend time actively away from your house without electronic devices. Go for a walk in a park, travel to a different city, swim in the sea, go to the mountains, take a bike ride, visit a concert or make a barbeque with friends.

8. Increase amount of positive thoughts

To spend most of the time in a good mood and in a high-performance state make a conscious decision to see the world through positive glasses. To increase the amount of positive thoughts that come to your head every morning think about 5 good things in your life that you are grateful for, schedule positive experiences in the future that you can anticipate, celebrate small successes that you have made within a day.

9. Live in a present moment

When you work, attempt to not think about future or past problems and concentrate on a present moment. A habit of living in a present moment not only improves productivity, but also boosts happiness by 11%.

10. Rule of 100 smiles

Smiling improves mood by releasing 3 types of feel-good hormones to the bloodstream: endorphins, dopamine and serotonin. Give yourself a goal to smile at least 100 times per day and your mood and energy will be on a very high level.

Each idea that you have learned in the *Insane Energy for Lazy People* system will allow you to noticeably increase your energy, however if you implement most of them you will significantly change your quality of life for the better. Ask yourself: "What actions will I take today to become more energetic?"

The most important thought

Imagine a boy by the name of Jack Jr. who is 10 years old and the same boy as an adult, now known as Jack Sr., who is 45 years old. Jack Jr. is significantly more energetic than Jack Sr. What do you think Jack Sr. would answer if you asked him: "Jack Sr., why you are significantly less energetic than Jack Jr.?" Most probably he would say: "Of course I am less energetic because I am older. My age is the main reason why I am less energetic." However the true reason why Jack Sr. is less energetic than Jack Jr. is the *Insane Energy for Lazy People* system.

Who exercises more, Jack Jr. or Jack Sr.? Of course Jack Jr. exercises more because he not only attends sports classes like boxing, dancing or swimming but also leads a significantly more active lifestyle. Jack Jr. plays football, basketball and baseball with his friends and spends a lot of time outside. Jack Sr. most probably works the entire day and leads a sedentary lifestyle.

Who eats more healthy food? Of course Jack Jr. eats more healthy food because his mother cares about his nutrition and makes sure that he eats enough fruits and vegetables. Jack Sr. is stressed at work and might eat comfort food like pizzas and hamburgers and drink alcohol.

Who is having a better sleep? Jack Jr. sleeps enough hours every night and goes to bed and wakes up at the same time every day. Jack Sr. might not sleep enough hours because he might need to finish important work at night or wake up early to attend an important meeting.

Who is having a perfect weight? Jack Jr. has obviously a perfect weight because he exercises, eats healthy food, sleeps better and has a better metabolism. Jack Sr. is most probably overweight because he works a lot and doesn't apply effort to maintain a perfect weight.

Who is smiling more? Jack Jr. is smiling more, enjoys life and has fun. Jack Sr. is serious, wants to look professional and smiles significantly less often.

Who is making more progress towards a goal? Jack Jr. makes more progress because he makes progress at school by becoming better in each subject, he makes progress in boxing, dancing or swimming classes, he makes progress in everything. Jack Sr. most probably does exactly the same work he has done for years and doesn't make any progress at all.

Who has better social connections? Jack Jr. has significantly better social connections: he has a big family with which he communicates, he has many friends, he is surrounded by many students and teachers at school. Jack Sr. mostly interacts with his wife, because his children have grown up and call him once a month, he lost connection with his past friends and didn't find new ones, and at work he has rare and brief interaction with colleagues.

Who is resting better on weekends and on vacations? Of course Jack Jr. not only has more weekends and holidays, but he also spends them very actively. Jack Sr. is working often on weekends or trying to solve some household problems and rarely takes vacations.

Who has a more positive outlook on life? Jack Jr. is looking forward to many positive events like going to the movies, playing a computer game or eating an ice cream, and he enjoys simple pleasures of life. Jack Sr. is not noticing simple pleasures of life and is thinking a lot about his failures from the past or problems that await him in future.

Here is the most important thought. Jack Sr. is doing significantly worse on all elements of the *Insane Energy for Lazy People* system compared to Jack Jr. He is blaming his age for not being energetic. The problem is that when people grow up they significantly change their lifestyle compared to the lifestyle they had in childhood and as a result their energy drops significantly. If you implement most of the ideas from the *Insane Energy for Lazy People* system you will be able to experience the same or higher level of energy as you experienced when you were 10 years old. Wouldn't it be awesome?

What to read next?

If you liked this book, you will also like *The Business Idea Factory: A World-Class System for Creating Successful Business Ideas.* Principles described in this book will allow you to effectively create successful business ideas and make your life more adventurous.

Another interesting book is *Magic of Impromptu Speaking: Create a Speech That Will Be Remembered for Years in Under 30 Seconds.* In this book, you will learn how to be in the moment, speak without preparation and always find the right words when you need them.

I also highly recommend you to read *Magic of Public Speaking: A Complete System to Become a World Class Speaker.* By using this system, you can unleash your public speaking potential in a very short period of time.

Biography

At the age of 19, Andrii obtained his CCIE (Certified Cisco Internetwork Expert) certification, the most respected certification in the IT world, and became the youngest person in Europe to hold it.

At the age of 23, he joined an MBA program at one of the top 10 MBA schools in the USA as the youngest student in the program, and at the age of 25 he joined Cisco Systems' Head Office as a Product Manager responsible for managing a router which brought in $1 billion in revenue every year.

These and other experiences have taught Andrii that success in any endeavor doesn't as much depend on the amount of experience you have but rather on the processes that you are using. Having dedicated over 10 years to researching behavior of world's most successful people and testing a variety of different techniques, Andrii has uncovered principles that will help you to unleash your potential and fulfill your dreams in a very short period of time.

The Business Idea Factory

A World-Class System for Creating Successful Business Ideas

The Business Idea Factory is an effective and easy-to-use system for creating successful business ideas. It is based on 10 years of research into idea-generation techniques used by the world's best scientists, artists, CEOs, entrepreneurs and innovators. The book is entertaining to read, has plenty of stories and offers bits of wisdom necessary to increase the quantity and quality of ideas that you create multiple times. Once you begin applying strategies described in this book, you will create successful business ideas regularly and make your life more adventurous. You will realize that there are few things that can bring as much joy and success in business as the moment when an excellent idea comes to your head.

Magic of Impromptu Speaking

Create a Speech That Will Be Remembered for Years in Under 30 Seconds

Magic of Impromptu Speaking is a comprehensive, step-by-step system for creating highly effective speeches in under 30 seconds. It is based on research of the most powerful techniques used by winners of impromptu speaking contests, politicians, actors and successful presenters. The book is entertaining to read, has plenty of examples and covers the most effective tools not only from the world of impromptu speaking but also from acting, stand-up comedy, applied psychology and creative thinking.

Once you master the system, you will grow immensely as an impromptu public speaker, become a better storyteller in a circle of friends and be more creative in everyday life. Your audience members will think that what you do on stage after such short preparation is pure magic and will recall some of your speeches many years later.

Magic of Public Speaking

A Complete System to Become a World Class Speaker

The Magic of Public Speaking is a comprehensive step-by-step system for creating highly effective speeches. It is based on research from the top 1000 speakers in the modern world. The techniques you will learn have been tested on hundreds of professional speakers and work! You will receive the exact steps needed to create a speech that will keep your audience on the edge of their seats. The book is easy to follow, entertaining to read and uses many examples from real speeches. This system will make sure that every time you go on stage your speech is an outstanding one.